FAGEOL & TWIN COACH BUSES
1922 THROUGH 1956
PHOTO ARCHIVE

William A. Luke

Iconografix
Photo Archive Series

Iconografix
PO Box 446
Hudson, Wisconsin 54016 USA

Library of Congress Card Number: 2002104767

ISBN 1-58388-075-5

02 03 04 05 06 07 08 5 4 3 2 1

Printed in China

Cover and book design by Shawn Glidden

Copyediting by Suzie Helberg

COVER PHOTO: The Twin Coach Corporation introduced a series of new bus models in 1946. The 34-S was one of the models. Pictured is a 34-S model carefully restored by the Monterey-Salinas Transit System of Monterey, California. See page 111 for more details about this Twin Coach.

BOOK PROPOSALS

Iconografix is a publishing company specializing in books for transportation enthusiasts. We publish in a number of different areas, including Automobiles, Auto Racing, Buses, Construction Equipment, Emergency Equipment, Farming Equipment, Railroads & Trucks. The Iconografix imprint is constantly growing and expanding into new subject areas.

Authors, editors, and knowledgeable enthusiasts in the field of transportation history are invited to contact the Editorial Department at Iconografix, Inc., PO Box 446, Hudson, WI 54016.

TABLE OF CONTENTS

ACKNOWLEDGMENTS

Photographs in this book are from the bus history library of the author, William A. Luke, unless noted as photo credits from other individuals and organizations.

The following persons and organizations were very helpful in providing information that has made this book possible.

Tom Jones, Librarian, Motor Bus Society, Clark, New Jersey

Loring M. Lawrence, Editor, Bus Industry, Manchester, New Hampshire

Paul A. Leger, President, Bus History Association, Halifax, Nova Scotia

Frank van den Boogert, Stichting Veteraan Autobussen, Lleidschenlinden, Netherlands

Special mention should also be made to acknowledge the late Tom Van De Grift, who, for a number of years, presented many photographs (some of which are used in this book) to the library of William A. Luke and others.

INTRODUCTION

Fageol is a very significant name in the history of bus manufacturing. The name belonged to the Fageol brothers who, at an early age, had a keen interest in motor vehicles.

Frank R. Fageol and William B. Fageol were innovators. One of their first ventures was selling automobiles in the San Francisco area. Later they became involved in building trucks, tractors and even automobiles, although only two autos were built. But their truck-building enterprise was quite successful, with a factory in Oakland, California being acquired in 1917.

In 1922, the Fageol brothers recognized that there was a need for a specially designed vehicle for the bus industry. Buses at that time were stretched automobile touring cars or passenger-carrying bodies mounted on truck chassis. These early buses were not entirely suitable for carrying passengers. They were uncomfortable and accidents were frequent. The Safety Coach, the first purpose-built vehicle for the bus industry, was the new product introduced by the Fageol brothers.

With its floor less than two feet above the roadway, the Fageol Safety Coach had a low center of gravity. The first models accommodated 22 passengers seated in rows across the width of the bus body. There was a door for each row of seats. An interesting identifying feature was the louvers across the top of the hood.

The Hall-Scott Company, an engine builder in Oakland, built the 4-cylinder engines for the first Safety Coaches. The bus was an immediate success. Not only were companies in California eager to purchase the Safety Coach, but also bus companies in Colorado, Minnesota, and elsewhere ordered Safety Coaches.

William Fageol was the engineer and Frank Fageol was the salesman, and the combination worked extremely well. Attractive literature, sales promotions and presentations at bus conventions all helped sell the Safety Coach.

Changes were made in the years following the introduction. A 6-cylinder Hall-Scott engine was featured soon afterward. The original Safety Coach was designed for intercity services. A "streetcar" model was introduced soon after the intercity model. Many cities became interested in the streetcar design, and sales of this type of bus were good. The air-braking system featured on the streetcar model in late 1922 was believed to be the first bus application of air brakes.

In 1923, the Fageol brothers brought bus production east to Cleveland, Ohio and the bus building business there was known as Fageol Motors of Ohio. A plant in Kent, Ohio was purchased the following year. Fageol buses were being built in both Oakland and Kent.

More changes and improvements were made to the Safety Coach, including a single entrance door at the front, a center aisle and increased headroom for the intercity buses. The streetcar body design originated with a single front door and high headroom.

The American Car & Foundry (ACF) Company of Philadelphia, Pennsylvania, acquired Fageol Motors Company of Ohio in Kent as well as Hall-Scott Motors. The Oakland Fageol Motors Company, which at that time was primarily owned by Louis Bill, was not a part of the transaction. In 1934, the Oakland factory and business assumed the name Fageol Truck and Coach Company though Frank and William Fageol had joined ACF several years earlier.

After some dispute primarily caused by ACF's lack of interest in new ideas presented by the Fageol brothers, the two resigned. They acquired Fageol Motors of Ohio and the Kent factory from ACF, and immediately began work on one of their ideas and in 1927 they had a prototype 40-passenger dual-engine bus. It was named Twin Coach, and the company became the Twin Coach Corporation.

The new Twin Coach bus was primarily built for city service, and was a big success. It was known originally as Model 100, but later became universally known as the Model 40. The timing was right, because many streetcar operating companies were looking for alternatives. A group of operators remarked at a gathering, "Every president and manager owes it to his property to test this vehicle against his traffic demands."

The new Twin Coach, like the Safety Coach introduced five years earlier, appealed to both the operating companies and the riding public. It had two Waukesha engines, one on each side. Engines built by the Hercules Engine Company later replaced the Waukesha units. More than 1,000 of the dual-engined Model 40 buses were built until production of that model ended in 1934. Many units acquired by transit companies saw service for years, some operating daily and providing important service during World War II.

A number of cities were establishing trolley bus routes in the early 1930s, and the 30-foot Model 40 Twin Coach body was built as a trolley bus to meet the demands of that time. Chicago (Illinois) Surface Lines bought 51 of the 83 Model 40 trolley buses that were built.

The Model 40 Twin Coach was also offered as an intercity coach, but the intercity model proved less popular than the city model. A streetcar using the Model 40 body was introduced, but this vehicle drew little or no interest.

Some of the Model 40 Twin Coach buses had gas-electric drives, but most had two gasoline engines and mechanical transmissions. Each engine had a driveline to the rear axle. It was reported that synchronizing the two engines was a challenge at that time.

The era of the small bus came in the early 1930s to answer the demand of a number of urban bus systems. The Twin Coach Corporation introduced several small bus models. These models seated 15, 19 and 20 passengers, but by far the most popular was the Model 30. The Model 30 looked like a smaller Model 40, but the single engine was mounted inside in the front next to the driver. Like that of the Model 40, the entrance door of the Model 30 was ahead of the front axle. Seating was for 30 passengers.

A Model 23S was introduced in 1934 and sold for three years. It also had a single Hercules engine mounted in the front, but with the front axle forward and the entrance door behind it. At the same time there was a need for large buses in the industry, and the Model 37R with a transversally rear-mounted Hercules gasoline engine was unveiled. A larger Model 40R with a greater seating capacity followed.

Later that year, Twin Coach built a new style trolley bus. At first, a 40-passenger trolley bus was built, followed by a 44-passenger model and a single articulated vehicle. Seattle (Washington) Transit System was the main purchaser of these trolley buses. In the early 1940s a total of 135 of these trolley buses were ordered by Seattle, marking the largest order of any trolley buses in the United States prior to World War II.

The Fageol brothers also tried to market a lightweight streetcar using the Model 40 body. Only four were built and it was found they were not accepted by the transit industry. However, a fairly successful venture for manufacturing small delivery trucks was established.

Another Twin Coach innovation came in 1935 when Models 23R, 27R and 30R were launched. The unique feature of these buses was the position of the Hercules engine. It was mounted over the rear axle, which was at the very end of the bus. The driveline from the transmission was positioned down to the rear axle.

The fact that there was no wheel housing or differential to require the floor of the bus be raised resulted in a flat floor and a small step for the passenger to enter or exit the bus. The 23R bus could be considered the first low floor bus. The Model 23R proved to be the most popular pre-World War II Twin Coach. A total of 1,271 were built.

Larger model Twin Coach buses made an appearance at the same time. They were the Models 31R, 35R, 40RC and 41AR with some variations. They had a transversally mounted gasoline engine with a forward driveline to the rear axle. These models sold very well, but mainly to larger cities.

Twin Coach had another first when it equipped a Model 37RDE bus with a diesel engine. Although previous buses were retrofitted with diesel engines, this was the first factory-built, diesel-engined bus. It went into service for the Eastern Massachusetts Street Railway of Boston, Massachusetts in July 1935. The bus had an electric drive and a Hercules DRXB diesel engine. One more diesel-electric bus was built, but a preference for gasoline engines continued.

Yet another innovation came from Twin Coach in 1938: a four-axle articulated bus seating 58 passengers, known as the Super Twin. It had a 6-cylinder Hercules diesel engine under the floor in the rear section. The drive was electric. The bus could bend vertically but not horizontally. One of the two built was sold to Baltimore (Maryland) Transit. A trolley bus version with three axles was built in 1940 as a demonstrator and sold to Cleveland Transit in 1942.

Gravity suspension was another new feature Twin Coach presented for its buses in 1939. Virtually all pre-World War II Twin Coach models had gravity suspension after 1939. This new suspension had the advantage of giving passengers a smoother ride. It was an invention by Truck Equipment Co. of Buffalo, New York, and used on Twin Coach buses under license.

In 1940, a longer Twin Coach accommodating 44 seated passengers was built. It was first known as the Model 44L, but soon afterward it was designated the 44G. Almost all of these buses built were diesel-electric.

During World War II, Twin Coach's Kent, Ohio plant was in production for the war effort and no buses were built. On August 15, 1944, a new line of post-war Twin Coach models was announced. There would be five models: 34-S, 38-S, 41-S, 41-D and 44-D. The "S" denoted a single engine and the "D" dual engines. The number indicated the seating capacity. When actual production began, the 41-D was dropped but the 44-D was built with two engines.

The post-war Twin Coach models had a new design featuring an under-floor engine location, a six-piece windshield, new window design with decorative aluminum sheeting on the side, and other features. Although Twin Coach had built many pre-war buses with diesel engines, gasoline engines were the choice for the new buses. Fageol Products Company was set up to build the engines. Suspension for the post-war Twin Coaches was the Goodrich Torsilastic suspension based on rubber. Spicer torque converters were standard on all new Twin Coach models.

A plant in Cheektowaga, New York was acquired and some of the post-war Twin Coach buses were built there. Also, assembly of buses for Canadian customers was established in Fort Erie, Ontario. All buses sold well. In 1947, 2,279 units were built, the 41-S being the most popular. The dual-engined Model 44-D Twin Coach did not fare as well, and in 1947 a larger engine known as the Model 44-S was designed for the 44-passenger bus. The 202 Model 44-D buses built were converted to single-engine buses.

The window design on the original post-war Twin Coach models was not satisfactory, and in 1948 a smaller window design was substituted on all models. The 50-S model was introduced at the same time, but only one was built. In 1950, the 52-S was announced, and it proved more popular. The Chicago Transit Authority purchased 500 of the new model. A 52-S2P Model designation was assigned to these propane-powered buses.

Twin Coach did not forget trolley buses or articulated buses in the post-war period. The Model 58-D articulated bus was announced in 1945, but none were built until 1948. Omaha & Council Bluffs Street Railway purchased 15 new Super Twin buses, beginning with an order for five in 1948. One of the Model 58-D bodies was built as a Highway Post Office. The body design for the post-war articulated bus was the same as all the post-war buses, but the articulation was only vertical like the pre-war Super Twin buses. One other Super Twin was produced, but was rebuilt as a trolley bus and sold to the Chicago (Illinois) Transit Authority.

In 1949, 154 Twin Coach trolley buses were ordered, 90 Model TTW units for the San Francisco (California) Municipal Railway and 60 for the Detroit (Michigan) Street Railway. Four Twin Coach trolley buses were exported to Belo Horizonte, Brazil.

A post-war Twin Coach intercity model bus was built especially for American Buslines in March 1947. American Buslines had planned to invest in a large fleet of these luxury buses, which had two 180-horsepower gasoline engines. Difficulties experienced by American Buslines following the delivery of this prototype were the main cause of the intercity bus program's demise. A single-engined intercity bus was built as well, but it also failed to generate enthusiasm in the bus industry marketplace.

A number of post-war Twin Coach buses were exported. Brazil, Netherlands, Turkey and Switzerland were among the countries bringing Twin Coach buses into service.

Diesel engines for buses became very popular in the early 1950s, and because Twin Coach had made the choice of using gasoline engines in post-war models, Twin Coach bus sales declined. Attempts were made to improve Twin Coaches, but diesel engines could not be properly fitted to the post-war Twin Coach models. Production of these post-war Twin Coaches ceased after 1951, with a total of 5,452 units built.

In 1952 and 1953, the Fageoliner bus series was introduced, but production ended after 155 units were built. Twin Coach received a contract for 500 military buses that could be converted from a 32-passenger bus to an ambulance or truck, or used as a combination passenger and cargo vehicle. A total of 1,546 of these vehicles were built.

In late 1952, the Flxible Company in Loudonville, Ohio, took over the production of Twin Coach transit buses and had the exclusive use of the Twin Coach name for a period of 10 years. Buses produced at the Flxible Loudonville plant carried the Flxible-Twin Coach name and nameplate. A large order from Chicago Transit Authority for 900 propane buses kept Flxible busy for seven years. Winnipeg Transit and Calgary Transit in Canada ordered some Flxible Twin Coach buses.

The story of the Fageol brothers and Twin Coach is an important part of the history of the bus industry in the United States. Frank and William Fageol gave the bus industry many innovations that helped the bus industry grow and prosper in its exciting development stages.

Fageol Safety Coach Buses

Pictured here is the prototype Fageol Safety Coach, introduced in January 1922. The engine used in this bus was a 4-cylinder, 50-horsepower Hall-Scott engine built especially to Fageol's specifications. Several changes were made before production began. The 4-cylinder engine was retained, seating was increased to 22 passengers and baggage was accommodated in the rear. The Safety Coach name was used because the bus designed by Fageol had a low center of gravity and had both front and rear axles equal in width. *Motor Bus Society*

One of the first companies to buy Fageol Safety Coaches was the White Bus Company. These early Safety Coach buses, built in 1922, had single tires and accommodated 14 passengers. A 4-cylinder Hall-Scott engine was used. Orville Caesar—who later became president of the Greyhound Corporation—established White Bus Company, originally headquartered in Superior, Wisconsin.

Mesaba Transportation Company, which began operating buses in Hibbing, Minnesota, in 1914, operated several Fageol Safety Coach buses when they first became available. The Safety Coaches like the one pictured here in 1922, operated on the Hibbing-Duluth route. It was a 16-passenger bus with a 4-cylinder Hall-Scott engine and a boot at the rear for baggage. Larger Fageol Safety Coach buses were acquired later. Mesaba Transportation eventually evolved into Greyhound Lines.

As Orville Caesar's White Bus Company expanded, it pioneered a route northeast of Duluth, Minnesota, to the Canadian cities of Fort William and Port Arthur, Ontario (both comprise the city known today as Thunder Bay) in 1924. This Fageol bus, built at the Oakland, California, factory had a 6-cylinder Hall-Scott engine and dual rear wheels. A number of northern Minnesota's pioneer bus companies were among the best customers for the Fageol Safety Coach.

Interstate Transportation Company, one of the early Minnesota bus companies, operated from Minneapolis west to Marshall, Minnesota. Northland Transportation Company acquired the company in 1925. These Fageol Safety Coach buses (one pictured here), built in Oakland, California, were bought by Interstate in 1923. The buses had 4-cylinder Hall-Scott engines and were able to seat 20 passengers. There were doors on the right side for each row of seats.

Jefferson Highway Transportation Company of Minneapolis, Minnesota, which began in 1919, operated Fageol Safety Coach buses. This 1926 Fageol is shown on a gravel road between Rochester, Minnesota, and the Twin Cities of Minneapolis and St. Paul. Edgar F. Zelle acquired Jefferson Highway Transportation Company in 1925, when the company had routes north and south of the Twin Cities. Zelle sold the northern routes to Northland Transportation Company and expanded the Jefferson routes south into Iowa.

The Purple Swan Safety Coach Lines began in 1926 with 20 Fageol Safety Coach buses in its fleet. These buses were 29-passenger models with Hall-Scott 6-cylinder engines. The Purple Swan main route was from Chicago to Kansas City via St. Louis. Because this route was an important link for transcontinental bus service, the company was in existence only a short time, being acquired by Pickwick Lines in 1927. This photo was taken in Boonville, Missouri.

14

Jack Rabbit Transportation Company got its start in Sioux Falls, South Dakota, in 1922. One of its first buses was this 1924 Fageol Safety Coach bus. By that time Fageol Motors Company had lengthened the chassis of the Safety Coach to 230 inches for the wheelbase, and had a sedan door in the front and an aisle between the seat rows. The Safety Coach was powered by a 6-cylinder Hall-Scott engine.

In its refinement of the Safety Coach, Fageol Motors Company lengthened the body to accommodate more passengers. Each row of seats continued to have a door on the right side. This Fageol Safety Coach was one of the buses operated by Citizen Auto Stage, a Nogales, Arizona-based pioneer bus company founded in 1916. Tom Morgan, Sr. bought the line in 1925, and his son, Tom, became president of the company in 1954.

Pictured here is one of the early Fageol Safety Coach deck-and-a-half buses. Spokane, Washington-based Auto Interurban Company, the origins of which can be traced to 1911, was the owner of this bus. Auto Interurban operated a number of local and long-distance routes from Spokane.

Fageol Motors Company had established a factory in Cleveland, Ohio, in the early 1920s, but by 1924 buses like this Safety Coach were being produced in Kent, Ohio. This 29-passenger intercity Safety Coach was built for the Wisconsin Power and Light Company, popularly known as the "Orange Line." This type of Safety Coach had a 6-cylinder Hall-Scott engine. The Orange Line operated extensive bus service in central Wisconsin, with a main route between Madison and Green Bay. The Orange Line was sold to Northland Greyhound Lines in 1935. *Motor Bus Society*

This Fageol Safety Coach bus operated by Jefferson Highway Transportation Company was unique because it was the only Safety Coach with a body built by Eckland Brothers of Minneapolis, Minnesota. The bus, which entered Jefferson service in 1927, had a center aisle and seated 21 passengers. Note the large enclosed boxes on the top of the bus for luggage. In 1927, Jefferson was operating these Fageol buses between Minneapolis/St. Paul and Mason City, Iowa, and also to Rochester, Minnesota.

In 1928, larger Fageol Safety Coach buses were built at the Oakland, California, factory. They were known as the Model 80 and had 25-passenger bodies and Waukesha engines. Columbia Gorge Motor Coach System of Portland, Oregon, bought three of the Model 80 Safety Coaches in June 1929. The company had a main route between Portland and Salt Lake City, Utah. Several cities in Washington State were also served.

The original Fageol factory in Oakland, California, is where the Safety Coach was first produced in 1922. The factory was new for Fageol Motors Company in 1917 and was originally used for the production of trucks and tractors. This Oakland plant continued to build some buses until 1938. *Motor Bus Society*

Fageol Safety Coach Streetcar-type Buses

Although the Fageol Safety Coach was originally built for intercity service, the Fageol brothers did not overlook the possibility of building city buses. In late 1922, the Puget Sound International Railway & Power Company bought eight of these Safety Coach buses to replace streetcars in Everett, Washington. One of these eight buses was reportedly the first bus to be equipped with air brakes. *Motor Bus Society*

After the first Fageol Safety Coach was introduced for highway service in early 1922, the "streetcar" type bus was launched to attract cities to buy the new Safety Coach buses. The "streetcar" type Safety Coach buses had a 218-inch chassis, 4-cylinder Hall-Scott engine, spoked wheels and hard rubber tires. San Diego (California) Electric Railway Company bought two Fageol Safety Coach buses in November 1922 to begin its first bus route. *Motor Bus Society*

The Public Service Corporation of New Jersey came into existence in 1903, and at the time operated a number of streetcar lines throughout New Jersey. By 1923, Public Service Transportation Company became a subsidiary of the Public Service Corporation, and bus service began. Two of the first buses were these 1923 Fageol city buses with so-called streetcar-type bodies. Arched upper windows and a special door for the driver were special features of these buses. Although Public Service's bus fleet grew, only a small number of Fageol buses were acquired. A review of the Public Service bus roster shows that no Twin Coach buses were ever purchased. *Motor Bus Society*

When the Georgia Railway and Power Company of Atlanta (Georgia) needed buses to serve certain routes of the expanding city, Fageol Motors Company was contacted for buses. The double-deck, 60-passenger buses were built with the combined efforts of Georgia Railway and Power Company, Fageol, and General Electric Company. General Electric provided the motors and generators for the gas-electric drive. The 15 Fageol double-deck buses, operated under the power company's Atlanta Coach Company subsidiary, entered service in September 1925.

In 1924, Fageol began using 6-cylinder, 73-horsepower Hall-Scott engines, enabling the company to offer double-deck buses. The Los Angeles (California) Motor Bus Company ordered two on an experimental basis. They proved satisfactory, and 32 more Fageol buses were added to the fleet. The buses featured air brakes, but only on the rear wheels. The upper deck was open. Los Angeles Motor Bus Company began operations in 1923.

This 1926 21-passenger Fageol Safety Coach was the only unit of this model in the Los Angeles (California) Railway Company fleet. Also in 1926, Los Angeles Railway Company added 20 larger 29-passenger Fageol Safety Coaches similar to this 21-passenger model. Los Angeles Railway Company began operating Fageol Safety Coach buses in 1923, and there were more than 60 in service in the 1920s, including double-deck models. *Motor Bus Society*

Chicago (Illinois) Surface Lines was the first company to acquire the Model 40 Twin Coach (then known as the Series 100). Five units were purchased in August 1927 and three more the following year. This Model 40 and one other was added to the Chicago fleet in 1930. These two Twin Coach buses had double entrance doors. No further Model 40 Twin Coaches were delivered to Chicago Surface Lines, although 58 Model 40 Twin Coach trolley buses were purchased. *George Krambles Archives*

The Cincinnati (Ohio) Street Railway Company was one of the first companies to purchase the Model 40 Twin Coach bus (the Model 40 was originally known as the Series 100). It was August 1928 when these eight Twin Coach buses were delivered to Cincinnati. These new buses served the Western Hills High School District and it was said at the time that they saved $300,000 that a streetcar expansion would have cost.

Jamaica Buses, Inc., of Jamaica, New York, bought 29 Model 40 Twin Coach buses in August 1933. The Jamaica company was one of many companies operating Model 40 buses. Approximately 1,200 units were built and sold to many city bus companies between 1927 and 1934, when production ceased. Jamaica Buses served the New York City area.

Four Model 40 Twin Coach buses were purchased by the Jacksonville (Florida) Traction Company in May 1929. The buses were assigned to an express schedule between Avondale-Murray Hill and downtown Jacksonville. The Model 40 buses were built from 1927 through 1934 with more than half of the 1,200 built in the first three years of production. The Jacksonville Traction Model 40 Twin Coaches were the first four buses that went into service for the company. Until 1941, Jacksonville had all Twin Coaches except one Yellow Coach bus.

This picture shows a part of the fleet of 34 Model 40 Twin Coach buses purchased by the Northern Ohio Power & Light Company in June 1929 for operation in Akron, Ohio. These buses were in service for a number of years and were operated by the Akron Transportation Company when that company became the operator of Akron transit routes. The Model 40 Twin Coach buses were introduced in 1927. They had a length of 31 feet 6 inches, and weighed 13,000 pounds.

The Milwaukee (Wisconsin) Railway and Light Company purchased six of these Model 40 Twin Coach buses in March 1931. They were painted green instead of the standard orange of the company. The green Milwaukee buses were assigned to special routes and used the Wisconsin Motor Bus Lines name. The Milwaukee Railway and Light Company bought its first two Model 40 Twin Coach buses in 1927. A total of 52 Model 40 Twin Coach buses were in service in Milwaukee, and some ran until 1949.

The Model 40 Twin Coach bus was made available with a gas-electric drive. Ten of these gas-electric Twin Coach buses were delivered to the Boston (Massachusetts) Elevated Railway in August 1928. There were only 21 gas-electric Model 40 Twin Coach buses built. Shown here is one of these buses, which went to Boston. The gas-electric buses featured ventilating louvers on the middle right side between the axles.

In 1930, a tunnel was built under the Detroit River connecting Detroit, Michigan and Windsor, Ontario. The Detroit & Canada Tunnel Corporation operated the tunnel and the bus service through it. The original buses for the route were 30 Model 40 Twin Coach buses. The route was 1.35 miles and there was a 10-minute headway. Except for a short distance over city streets in Detroit, the service was entirely on the company's property. The Tunnel Corporation later bought a fleet of 34-S Twin Coach buses.

The Twin Coach Model 40 was also made available as an intercity bus beginning in 1929. It had a single door in the front and there were curtains in the windows. Another feature was grillwork in the back. There were approximately 132 built in the intercity version, but they were not as popular as the transit model. Some of the intercity Model 40 buses were reported to have lavatories.

Chicago (Illinois) Surface Lines was an operator of trolley buses beginning in 1930, and its first trolley buses were 29 Model 40 Twin Coach units. This Model 40 Twin Coach trolley bus was in the last group of 10 delivered in 1931; in fact, they were the last Twin Coach trolley buses bought by Chicago Surface Lines. However, Chicago had 52 of the 83 Model 40 Twin Coach trolley buses built between 1927 and 1934. *George Krambles Archives*

Duluth-Superior Transit Company of Duluth, Minnesota, purchased nine Model 40 Twin Coach trolley buses in July 1934. These were the last Model 40 trolley buses built by the Twin Coach Corporation. At the time Duluth-Superior Transit had 18 trolley buses and was one of the smaller cities operating trolley buses. Duluth-Superior Transit also operated several Twin Coach gasoline buses. *Motor Bus Society*

The Fageol brothers purchased this factory in Kent, Ohio, from ACF Motors Company in 1927, and production of the dual-engine Twin Coach began at the factory that year. This site was used for production of Twin Coach models until it was sold to the Flxible Corporation. After World War II, Twin Coach also built buses in Cheektowaga, New York. An assembly plant in Fort Erie, Ontario, assembled Twin Coach buses mainly for Canadian customers.

Twin Coach Corporation introduced the Model 30 bus in 1931. It was said to answer the demand for a bus seating 26 passengers. It had a Hercules WXR engine mounted in the front alongside the driver. This Model 30 was very popular, with 900 units built until 1935. The Kansas City (Missouri) Public Service Company bought 129 of the Model 30 and the larger Model 30A.

In June 1932, Triple Cities Traction Company of Binghamton, New York, discontinued its streetcars and substituted a fleet of 45 Twin Coach buses. There were 19 Model 20 buses shown in this picture and 26 Model 40 Twin Coach buses in this acquisition. Triple Cities Traction Company served Binghamton, Johnson City and Endicott, resulting in the "Triple Cities" name.

The smallest Twin Coach bus, the Model 15, had a 73-horsepower Hercules JXC engine. The Tennessee Electric Power Company acquired three Model 15 Twin Coach buses in May 1932 for service in Chattanooga, Tennessee. The buses were 19 feet 5 inches long and 69 inches wide. Approximately 50 Model 15 Twin Coach buses were built.

San Antonio, Texas, was reported to be the first large city in the United States to abandon streetcars for buses; this was in 1932. Pictured here is one of the 50 Model 19 Twin Coach buses acquired by the San Antonio Public Service Company to replace the streetcars. Small buses were the choice made by the company, but larger buses were added beginning in the late 1930s. Although San Antonio Public Service operated a variety of buses, Twin Coach buses were dominant in the fleet. *Motor Bus Society*

In May 1932, Auto Interurban Company of Spokane, Washington, bought three of these Model 15 Twin Coach buses for service in eastern Washington and Idaho. Auto Interurban, founded in 1913, was a good customer for Twin Coach buses as well as Fageol buses in earlier years.

Ten of these small Twin Coach buses were delivered to the Houston (Texas) Electric Company in 1930. This was an unusual Twin Coach, designated as Model 26. At the time, bus routes were expanding in fast-growing Houston. There were 24 Model 40 Twin Coach buses in the fleet with another 24 added later. Houston Electric Company abandoned streetcars in 1938 and subsequently incorporated a great number of bus makes. There were a sizable number of Twin Coach buses in the fleet until 1948. *Motor Bus Society*

The Pacific Electric Railway Company of Los Angeles, California, purchased nine streamlined Model 30-S Twin Coach buses in 1934. Pacific Electric Railway Company had an extensive transit system in the Los Angeles area, with more than 1,000 miles of electric railway track. It first began bus service in 1917, mainly as feeder routes and small urban services. The small Twin Coach Model 30-S buses were suitable for routes in Pasadena and other Los Angeles suburban communities. *Motor Bus Society*

The Model 23-S Twin Coach was made available in 1933 as a streamlined type similar to the successful Model 30. The Model 23-S had a Hercules JXDT engine mounted in the front, but unlike the Model 30, the entrance door was behind the front wheels. There were 238 buses of this type built, according to reports. Twin Coach's introduction of the Model 23-R in 1936 ended production of the Model 23-S.

A total of 15 of these Model 23-S Twin Coach buses were bought by the Duluth-Superior Bus Company of Duluth, Minnesota, between 1935 and 1937. These two-door buses were used for several years on an interstate route between Duluth, Minnesota, and Superior, Wisconsin, over the Interstate Toll Bridge. The buses were quite fast and they could make up time after waits when the bridge was opened up for ships.

The Twin Coach Corporation introduced the Model 30-AS bus in 1933. It was primarily designed for city transit service, but some intercity bus companies bought the Model 30-AS. Penn Ohio Coach Lines of Youngstown, Ohio, bought three in 1933, one of which is pictured here. Four more were added in 1934. Penn Ohio Coach Lines grew out of several electric railway companies in 1922. Greyhound Lines began acquiring an interest in Penn Ohio in 1943 and became a full owner of the company in 1946. *Motor Bus Society*

Twin Coach Corporation introduced the new Model 37-R bus, its first rear-engine model, in 1934. The engine, a 126-horsepower Hercules, was mounted transversally. The bus had a pointed front, which was later replaced with a flat front. Trenton (New Jersey) Transit Company was among the first to operate the 37-R buses and had 25 of them delivered in 1935.

The St. Louis (Missouri) Public Service Company operated many makes of buses. Various Twin Coach models were included, with the first being Model 40s acquired in 1928. Shown here is one of the 28 Twin Coach Model 37-R buses bought in 1935 and 1936. The St. Louis Public Service Company purchased no Twin Coach buses after 1935.

In July 1935, Twin Coach became the first bus manufacturer to install a diesel engine in a transit bus. The engine was a Hercules DKXB diesel, mounted transversally in the rear. The bus had an electric transmission. Eastern Massachusetts Street Railway Company of Boston, Massachusetts, bought the bus, which was designated as Model 37-RDE.

The New Orleans (Louisiana) Public Service Company purchased five of these Model 31-R Twin Coach buses in 1937. The Model 31-R had a Hercules WXRT gasoline engine, the same engine used in the Model 30-R Twin Coach. The Model 31-R had a 174 1/2-inch wheelbase compared with the Model 30-R's 235 1/2-inch wheelbase. With its tight turning ability, the 31-R was better suited for the narrow streets in some areas of the city. New Orleans Public Service only had 131 buses in 1937.

This was one of three Twin Coach Model 35-RDE buses that were operated by Gray Coach Lines, Ltd., Toronto, Ontario. Two were delivered in 1937 and the other in 1938. These buses were originally assigned to the T. Eaton Inter-Store service in downtown Toronto. The service was for customers wishing to visit both stores on their shopping trips. Gray Coach Lines had previously ordered Model 23-R Twin Coaches. *Motor Bus Society*

In December 1937 the Los Angeles (California) Railway acquired 10 Model 40-RC Twin Coach buses, the first of this type produced. These buses had a length of 239 1/2 inches. A Hercules RXCT engine was mounted transversally in the rear. The seating capacity was 40 passengers.

Twin Coach and Fageol were well known by intercity bus companies, and most Twin Coach models were adapted for intercity operations. Pictured here is a Model 35-GP Twin Coach, one of two built for Union Pacific Stages in 1940. It had a raised passenger deck and under-floor baggage lockers. Windows, which were fitted with curtains, were smaller than windows on the Model 35-R city buses. Union Pacific Stages operated services in the Pacific Northwest, but was linked with Interstate Transit Lines and Chicago Northwestern Stages forming a large bus system from Chicago and Kansas City to the West Coast. Union Pacific also had considerable local service in the Boise, Idaho and Spokane, Washington areas.

This Model 35-G Twin Coach was one of a five-bus order by the Akron (Ohio) Transportation Company delivered in 1941. These buses and most Twin Coach buses delivered after 1939 had "gravity suspension." It was the same as torsion-bar suspension, which was used on post-war Twin Coach buses. This suspension provided a very good ride for passengers whether the bus had a light load or was at full capacity. Another innovation was "standee" windows. Akron Transportation Company operated more than 100 Twin Coach buses.

Twin Coach Model 23R, 27R, 30R Buses

The Twin Coach Model 30-R and companion Model 23-R were introduced in 1935. These buses were built with monocoque construction, a first for any bus. The Hercules TC-320 engine was mounted above the rear wheels and the drive shaft was downward. Woodlawn & Southern Motor Coach Company received this Model 30-R Twin Coach and one other unit in March 1936. Two more were added the next year. Although Woodlawn & Southern operated most of its service in Aliquippa, Pennsylvania, in the Pittsburgh suburban area, the company was headquartered in Ambridge, Pennsylvania.

Tri-City Railways of Iowa, which operated buses in Davenport, Iowa, and Rock Island and Moline, Illinois, bought 16 of these Model 23-R Twin Coach buses in September 1936. The Model 23-R had its Hercules TC-320 gasoline engine mounted above the rear axle, resulting in minimum restrictions inside the bus and a flat, low floor.

The Winnipeg (Manitoba) Electric Company was a very good Twin Coach customer for many years. In May 1937, 10 of these Model 23-R Twin Coach buses were acquired. The Model 23-R was the most popular pre-World War II Twin Coach bus, with a total of 1,375 built. The Model 23-R Twin Coach was found in many cities throughout the United States and Canada.

Spokane (Washington) United Railways began operating service in 1922. In 1937, the company eliminated streetcars and became an all-bus operation. At the time there was a mixture of equipment, but Fargo buses dominated. Twin Coach buses were added to the fleet beginning in 1936, first with 24 Model 23-R buses and then two orders totaling 44 Model 30-R buses like No. 153, pictured here.

Los Angeles (California) Railway received nine Model 30-R Twin Coach buses in November 1935. The Model 30-R buses had a very long 235 1/2-inch wheelbase because the WXRT Hercules engine was mounted over the rear wheels. The length of the Model 30-R was 28 1/2 feet. The Los Angeles Model 30-R buses, seating 30 passengers, were among the first of this model delivered.

This rear view of the engine compartment of the Twin Coach Model 23-R shows the position of the Hercules TC-320 gasoline engine, mounted transversally above the rear axle. The Spicer transmission had a driveline downward to the rear axle. The radiator and fan were to the right. The bulkhead separating the passenger compartment had two windows similar to the slanted outer rear bodywork. It was a unique arrangement, but proved successful at that time for Twin Coach. *Motor Bus Society*

In 1940, Twin Coach rounded the upper windows in a styling change to models that were offered at that time. The Arkansas Power and Light Company of Little Rock, Arkansas, acquired 20 of these Model 27-GS buses in late 1940. They operated in Little Rock under the subsidiary company Capital Transportation Company. This photo was taken in Ohio before delivery to Little Rock.

Ashland & Shamokin Autobus Company of Mount Carmel, Pennsylvania, was formed in 1937 from the Shamokin & Mount Carmel Transit Company. The companies served a number of coal mining communities in central Pennsylvania. The company continues to operate today, but it is primarily involved in tours using the name King Coal Tours. The Model 30-GS Twin Coach pictured was purchased in 1942. It was one of the first small Twin Coach buses to have a slanted windshield. Also it had one door, a feature generally used by companies operating local intercity routes. "Standee" windows were another new feature for Twin Coach buses at that time.

The Youngstown (Ohio) Municipal Railway had the second largest Twin Coach pre-war trolley bus fleet, with 54 Model 42-RTT and Model 44-GTT vehicles. Youngstown's trolley bus system, which began in 1936, had only Twin Coach trolley buses until 1946. *Motor Bus Society*

Seattle (Washington) Transit System enthusiastically began a trolley bus system in 1940, replacing streetcars. The Twin Coach Corporation was one of two builders to receive Seattle's order for trolley buses (the other was Brill). Seattle ordered 135 Twin Coach trolley buses in 1940, the single largest order for trolley buses in the United States up to that time. Pictured here is one of Seattle's Model 41-GWFT Twin Coach trolley buses.

In 1938, Twin Coach built the Super Twin, a four-axle articulated bus seating 58 passengers. It had a hinge in the middle of two units. Unlike most articulated buses, it did not bend horizontally, making it difficult for the bus to round corners. The Baltimore (Maryland) Transit Company acquired the Super Twin pictured here. A Hercules DRXB diesel engine was mounted in the rear of the bus. The bus weighed 28,000 pounds.

The smallest post-World War II Twin Coach was the Model 34-S, which had a seating capacity of 34 passengers with two doors. A Fageol Twin Coach 180-horsepower gasoline engine mounted under the floor powered the bus. A Spicer Hydraulic Torque Converter eliminated gear changing and Torsilastic suspension gave the bus a smooth ride. Tulsa (Oklahoma) City Lines was the owner of this Model 34-S. Tulsa City Lines was a National City Lines property, which normally did not purchase many Twin Coach buses.

Included in the new line of four Twin Coach city bus models was this Model 44-S, introduced in 1945. Indianapolis (Indiana) Railways, Inc., acquired this Model 44-S and nine others soon after they were made available. Ten more were bought a year later. These Twin Coach buses and five Model 34-S buses were the only Twin Coaches to operate in Indianapolis. The Model 44-S was originally designed with dual engines, but the dual engines proved unsatisfactory. As a result, Fageol's 451-cubic-inch, 200-horsepower under-floor engine was used for the Model 44-S.

70

The Milwaukee (Wisconsin) and Suburban Transport Company was a good Twin Coach customer for many years. In June 1949, 22 Model 41-SW Twin Coach buses were purchased. With a 102-inch-wide body, the Model 41-SW was different from the usual Model 41-S Twin Coach. Milwaukee also had 116 wide-bodied Model 34-SW Twin Coach buses, but these were ordered in 1947 and 1948 when the Milwaukee system was known as The Milwaukee Electric Railway & Transport Company.

The Twin Coach Model 58-DW was the post-World War II 60-foot Super Twin Coach. This model had two 180-horsepower engines mounted under the floor behind the front axle. Hydraulic torque converters were used. Intersteering allowed the 47-passenger bus to have a turning radius similar to a 35-foot, 10-inch bus. The articulated hinge allowed the body section to bend vertically, but not horizontally. The Omaha and Council Bluffs Street Railway of Omaha, Nebraska, bought 15 of these Super Twin Coaches, the first being delivered in 1948. There were 16 of these buses built and one trolley bus.

The United States Highway Post Office Service was established in July 1940. Mail was being carried by the trains and sorted on-board, but with the curtailment of a number of trains, the transportation and sorting of mail aboard the special buses was determined to be a viable substitute. The first route was operated in early 1941. There were about 400 routes established. The last route between Cleveland and Cincinnati, Ohio, was discontinued in 1974. The largest Highway Post Office bus, built in 1949, was a Model 58-D6 Super Twin Coach with two engines. It was probably operated in southern California.

This bus was named the Highway Luxury Liner and was for a proposed fleet of buses for American Buslines of Chicago, Illinois. Twin Coach built only one of these buses, which was designated as Model 360. It had two 180-horsepower Fageol-Twin Coach engines mounted longitudinally in the rear. Torsilastic suspension was another feature. The bus had seating for 37 passengers. Twin Coach planned to build a similar single-engine Luxury Liner for 29 passengers, but it was never built.

Pictured here is a rail bus—actually a Model 38-S Twin Coach—equipped with steel wheels for operating on railroad tracks. It also had a large headlight, horn and cowcatcher. The rail bus was built for Missouri Pacific Lines' suburban service in the Houston, Texas, area. A test bus was delivered in 1947, and five more were added in February 1948. Each vehicle cost $17,000. The service ended in 1961.

The Twin Coach Company built 154 post-war trolley buses designated as Model 48-TT2. The Detroit (Michigan) Street Railway Company acquired 60 of the trolley buses (one of which is shown here) in 1949, and the buses were used on the company's new Crosstown Line. San Francisco (California) Municipal Railway received 90 post-war Twin Coach trolley buses and four were exported to Belo Horizonte, Brazil.

Asbury Rapid Transit System of Los Angeles, California, purchased 16 Model 52-S2 Twin Coach buses—six in June 1950 and 10, including the one pictured, in October 1951. These buses were powered with propane engines and were the last Twin Coach buses built. The name Fageoliners was used for buses built by the Twin Coach Company in 1952 and 1953. Only 155 of the Fageoliners were built.

Somerset Bus Company of Mountainside, New Jersey, bought eight Model FS-40 Fageoliners in November 1952. They were in the last group of buses built by the Twin Coach Company. The Fageoliners, introduced in 1952, had the same body style as the post-war Twin Coach models. One variation was the addition of "standee" windows. Fageoliners came in five models, seating 33, 36, 40, 44 and 51 passengers. *Motor Bus Society*

The Twin Coach Company received a contract for 500 military coaches in 1950. These were called "Convertibles" because they could be changed from a 32-passenger bus to an 18-liter ambulance or a cargo-hauling truck. They were built in different configurations, and from all appearances, the 1,546 units built were very different looking from previous Twin Coach models. The box-like look probably was the result of them being built in conjunction with the Fruehauf Trailer Company of Detroit, Michigan. The "Convertible" pictured here in 1954 in Bethany, Missouri, was a Highway Post Office vehicle. A Fageol 6-cylinder engine was mounted under the floor.

The Twin Coach Fageoliner was built in April 1951. The six-piece windshield of the pre-war Twin Coach models was replaced with a rounded two-part windshield. This bus was built using Fruehauf Trailer Company parts. Leaf springs were used instead of the Torsilastic suspension employed on previous post-war Twin Coach models. The plan was to sell these buses at a much lower price than previous models. *Motor Bus Society*

The Twin Coach Company began working with the Flxible Company of Loudonville, Ohio, in 1952. Flxible was a builder of intercity buses, and like Twin Coach, was having difficulty selling buses in the early 1950s. The following year, Twin Coach transferred production of the Twin Coach-designed transit bus to Flxible, which was allowed to use the Twin Coach name for a 10-year period. Chicago (Illinois) Transit Authority, a loyal Twin Coach customer, continued purchasing the Flxible Twin Coach buses. Pictured here is one of about 1,000 Flxible Twin Coach Model FT2P-40 buses purchased by the Chicago Transit Authority.

Post-war Twin Coach Buses

Duluth-Superior Transit Company, Duluth, Minnesota, was a good Twin Coach customer beginning in 1931. This Model 34-S Twin Coach was one of the first post-war Twin Coaches built. It was delivered to Duluth in March 1946.

The Omaha and Council Bluffs Street Railway Company of Omaha, Nebraska, was a good Twin Coach customer operating most of the post-war Twin Coach models built. In the spring of 1947, Omaha took delivery of 30 Model 34-SW 102-inch-wide Twin Coach buses.

Fargo, North Dakota's Northern Transit Company bought six Model 38-S Twin Coach buses in late 1949.

This Model 34-S bought in August 1946 was the first of 12 Twin Coach buses operated by the Sioux City (Iowa) Transit Company.

Wisconsin Public Service Company, Green Bay, bought 10 Model 34-S Twin Coaches, one is pictured here in August 1947. Two others were acquired the previous year. Each Green Bay bus carried the motto "Ride the Public Service Streetliners."

Eau Claire (Wisconsin) had two Twin Coach Model 34-S buses in its fleet. One is pictured here.

Bluebird Coach Lines, Lyons, Illinois, bought 15 Model 34-S Twin Coaches in August 1948. Bluebird also had larger Twin Coaches including eight propane-powered 45-S models and six 52-S2 models in 1951. Bluebird operated suburban service in the Chicago area. *Motor Bus Society*

Pictured is one of the 500 Twin Coach Model 52-S2 buses delivered to the Chicago (Illinois) Transit Authority in late 1950 and into 1951. They were all propane-powered.

In 1947, Springfield (Illinois) Transportation Company added two Model 34-S Twin Coaches to its fleet. Six others had been acquired in 1946. The Model 34-S pictured here in 1948 is passing by the old Illinois State Capitol.

Fort Wayne (Indiana) Transit bought this Model 38-S Twin Coach and 14 others in June 1947. It was built at Twin Coach's Buffalo, New York, plant.

Kansas City (Missouri) Public Service Company bought 32 Model 34-S Twin Coaches in early 1947, one of which is pictured here. Kansas City was a good Twin Coach customer. It had purchased 164 pre-war Twin Coaches and 190 post-war Twin Coaches.

One of the smallest cities to operate Twin Coach buses was Boone, Iowa. Boone Bus Service bought this Model 38-S in December 1947.

In 1947, United Electric Railways, Providence, Rhode Island, bought 34 of the last Model 44-D dual-engined Twin Coaches built.

This Model 41-S Twin Coach was one of four purchased by Atlantic City (New Jersey) Transportation Company in June 1949. Atlantic City operated three other models of Twin Coach buses, including the last original post-war design models—five Model 45-S buses. Atlantic City Transportation had an unusual black-and-pale yellow livery. *Loring M. Lawrence*

In February and October 1951, Syracuse (New York) Transit Corporation acquired 20 of these Model 45-S Twin Coach buses.

Rochester (New York) Transit Corporation bought some of the first Model 38-S Twin Coaches. Ten, including this one, were added in July 1946. Three other orders followed.

Asbury Rapid Transit System of Los Angeles, California, added these Model 41-S Twin Coach buses and three others to its fleet in June 1947. Three more were added in 1948.

Pacific Electric Railway, Los Angeles, California, was one of about 30 companies which bought Model 44-D dual-engined Twin Coach buses. This Model 44-D was acquired with four others in 1946.

The Yakima (Washington) Transportation Company had eight post-war Twin Coaches; six were Model 34-S, two pictured here, and two were Model 38-S. The transit system in Yakima was owned by the Union Pacific Railroad, hence the "UP" shield on the front of the bus.

Boise (Idaho) Bus Company bought eight of these Model 34-S Twin Coach buses in 1946.

Garfield Heights (Ohio) Coach Lines, which bought the first Model 44-D Twin Coach, also bought two Model 45-S buses, one of which is shown here. These two were delivered in October 1951 and were among the last Model 45-S buses built.

Redifer Bus System, a small suburban bus line operated in the Cleveland, Ohio area, had a fleet of five Twin Coaches including this Model 38-S bought in 1946. Two more Model 38-S Twin Coaches came the next year. Redifer owned one of the first Fageoliner Model FL-35Ms and a Model FLD-40.

Tucson (Arizona) Rapid Transit Company added three of these Model 41-S Twin Coaches in November 1947. Three others were bought earlier that year.

Metropolitan Lines of Phoenix, Arizona, acquired this Twin Coach Model 34-S and two others in June 1946. An additional two others came in March 1946 and four more were added later. The company's official name was Menderson Bus Line.

This Model 41-S Twin Coach was in service for the Toronto (Ontario) Transportation Commission (TTC). Gray Coach Lines, a subsidiary of TTC, originally purchased it in June 1948.

Gray Coach Lines, Toronto, Ontario, had almost 50 Canadian-built Model 41-S Twin Coach buses in its fleet, like the one pictured here. Gray Coach also operated model 44-S Twin Coaches. All were purchased in 1948.

Canadian Pacific Transport Company of Preston, Ontario, had nine Model 38-S Twin Coaches in its fleet. This Model 38-S was delivered with five others in 1946. The Canadian Pacific Railway Company owned the Preston operation.

Hamilton (Ontario) Street Railway Company was the third owner of this Model 41-S Twin Coach. Erie Coach Line of Port Colborne, Ontario, originally acquired it in 1947. Canada Coach Line of Hamilton was the second owner of the bus.

The Dallas (Texas) Railway and Terminal Company bought 40 Model 38-S Twin Coaches in July and October 1947. These were the only post-war Twin Coach buses in the Dallas fleet.

Wichita (Kansas) Transportation Corporation acquired 15 of these Model 38-S Twin Coach buses in August 1947. Wichita had a large post-war Twin Coach fleet including 37 Model 34-S, 10 Model 41-S and 11 Model 38-SL buses.

Ottawa (Ontario) Transit Commission acquired 10 of these Model 44-S Twin Coach buses in December 1949 and January 1950. Five Model 45-S Twin Coaches were delivered to Ottawa in late 1950.

Quebec Central Transportation Company of Quebec City, Quebec, had five of these Model 41-S Twin Coach buses delivered in the summer of 1948. *Paul A. Leger Collection*

The Sandwich, Windsor & Amherstberg Railway Company, Windsor, Ontario, had a large fleet of Twin Coach buses. Ten of these Model 38-S Twin Coaches were added in early 1950.

The Detroit-Windsor Tunnel Corporation, Detroit, Michigan, which was an exclusive Twin Coach operator since it began in 1931, bought this Model 41-S Twin Coach in a 15-bus order in September 1947.

San Antonio (Texas) Transit Company acquired 30 Model FLP-35 Twin Coach Fageoliners in September and October 1952.

Belleville-St. Louis Coach Company of Belleville, Illinois, bought two of these Model 44-S Twin Coaches in 1950. The company operated interstate between Belleville, Illinois, and St. Louis, Missouri.

Georgia Power Company, Atlanta, Georgia, bought four of these Model 34-S Twin Coach buses in June 1947. Georgia Power had placed several orders earlier for Model 34-S Twin Coach buses for its Augusta, Georgia, operation. *Motor Bus Society*

Southern Coach Lines, operating in Chattanooga, Tennessee, acquired 40 of these Model 41-S Twin Coach buses in 1946 and 1947.

Edmonton (Alberta) Transit System added 13 Model 45-S Canadian-built Twin Coach buses in April 1951. Ten were also acquired in November 1950. They were all propane-powered.

British Columbia Hydro in Vancouver, British Columbia, was the operator of this Model 38-S Twin Coach. It was originally purchased in September 1947 by the British Columbia Electric Company, the predecessor company.

East Street Bus Line of Taunton, Massachusetts, bought this Model 38-S Twin Coach from the Boston, Worcester & New York Street Railway Company of Framingham, Massachusetts, which purchased it in October 1950.

Boston, Worcester & New York Street Railway Company (better known as The B&W Lines) of Framingham, Massachusetts, had a trio of Model 38-S Twin Coach buses in October 1951. Twin Coach did not build any more Model 38-S buses after this B&W order. *Loring M. Lawrence*

The Fitchburg and Leominster Street Railway Company of Fitchburg, Massachusetts, received six Twin Coach Fageoliner Model FL-30 buses in April 1952. They were among the first Fageoliner buses built. *Loring M. Lawrence*

This Model 34-S Twin Coach bus (No. 301) and three others entered the Utica (New York) Transit fleet in May 1946. Later that year 14 more were acquired. Utica Transit also had five Model 38-S Twin Coaches and three Model 44-S Twin Coaches. The Model 44-S buses were the last of that model. *Loring M. Lawrence*

Foreign-delivered Twin Coach Buses

The city of Belo Horizonte, Brazil, was the only foreign city to receive post-war Twin Coach trolley buses. Four of the Model 44-TTW Twin Coach trolley buses (one pictured here) entered service in Belo Horizonte in 1953. *Postcard, Allen Morrison Collection*

The large Brazilian long-distance bus operator Viacao Cometa of Sao Paulo acquired 42 post-war Twin Coach buses. This Model 41-SM was delivered to Viacao Cometa in late 1948. It is shown on the highway linking Sao Paulo with Santos.

This Model 40 Twin Coach was originally sold to the German bus manufacturer Bussing in 1929. In May 1930 Bussing sold it to the Berliner-Verkehrs VG. It was the only Twin Coach known to have operated in Berlin. *Fredrich Muller*

Five post-war Model 44-SDT Twin Coach buses were exported to Switzerland in 1948 and were operated by Verkehrsbetriebe Luzern in Luzern. This one is pictured in Luzern. *Jan Voerman*

This Model 41-S Twin Coach and two others were built in June 1947 and exported to Holland for the large Maarse and Kroon bus operation in Aalsmeer. Maarse and Kroon acquired five more Model 41-S Twin Coach buses later in 1947. *Jan Voerman*

A number of Twin Coach buses were exported to Turkey. This Model 34-S Twin Coach is seen on this post card operating at the waterfront in Izmir, Turkey. Izmir also had four Model 41-S Twin Coaches.

The Twin Coach name resurfaced in 1968 when a new small bus was introduced by Highway Products, Inc., a Kent, Ohio-based company founded by J. T. Myers. Myers had become a director of the Twin Coach Company in 1955. Highway Products had been building defense vehicles, highway post office vehicles, Compac-Vans and engines during the 1960s. Up until 1963, the Twin Coach name was used on transit buses built by the Flxible Corporation. The agreement for the use of the Twin Coach name ended at that time.

In 1968, when the small Twin Coach entered the marketplace, there was a renewed interest in transit because the federal government began offering grants for bus transportation. It was thought that there would be a demand for 25 31-passenger buses especially in small cities, in addition to other applications.

The first Highway Products' Twin Coach buses were 25-passenger models with Chrysler V-8 gasoline engines and automatic transmissions mounted in the rear of the bus. The model designation was known as the TC-25 and the Twin Coach emblem, similar to the one used on post-war Twin Coaches between 1946 and 1955, was used on the buses.

A "unitized" frame and body design said to be for maximum strength and safety was featured. The weight of the original Highway Products Twin Coach was 9,100 pounds. Brakes on original models were air over hydraulic, weatherproof with improved linings and components, but full air brakes were used. Leaf springs were used on the first models, but full air suspension was introduced in 1971.

The Detroit Diesel Model 4-53 diesel engine was offered on later models. A larger 31-passenger Highway Products Twin Coach was made available in the 1970s.

Highway Products experienced difficult times in the 1970s and the company closed its doors in late 1975 after approximately 900 units were built.

The Muskegon Transit Authority introduced ten of these Highway Products' Twin Coach Model T-31 buses in Muskegon, Michigan, in 1970. They replaced leased step vans that proved unsatisfactory for urban service. The buses were purchased by a local bank and then leased to the city with a provision that the Transit Authority could purchase them later.

A special bus service called Pert Dial-A-Bus was inaugurated to serve 30,000 residents of Greece, New York, a suburb of Rochester. A small fleet of these TC-25 Highway Products Twin Coach buses were acquired for this service.

Battle Creek (Michigan) Coach Company ordered 17 Highway Products Twin Coach buses in 1970. They went into city service in Battle Creek, replacing older buses. These new buses were 25-passenger models and had 383-cubic-inch Chrysler engines mounted in the rear.

Santa Clara County (California) Transit District was formed in November 1972. The center of the district was San Jose, a city of a half million persons at the time. The county required interurban services as well as urban transit. To operate a local transit service, 134 Highway Products Model TC-31B buses were acquired, one of which is pictured here.

Haddonfield, New Jersey, began a Dial-A-Ride service in February 1972 with 12 17-passenger Highway Products Twin Coach Model TC-25 buses. The Twin Coach buses were very suitable for Dial-A-Ride services, which were beginning to be launched in a number of areas. The buses were only 25-feet long and were able to easily serve in narrow residential streets.

A fleet of 15 medium-sized Highway Products Twin Coach buses went into service in 1972 by the District of Columbia Department of Highway and Traffic. The buses could operate on both liquefied natural gas and gasoline. An international Exposition of Transportation called Transpo-72 at Washington's Dulles Airport used the buses.

This Model TC-25 Highway Products Twin Coach went into service in early 1973 in Bridgeton, New Jersey. Garden State Coachways was the operator of the bus, which was purchased by the State of New Jersey Department of Transportation. It had a diesel engine. The bus served four routes each with a 15-minute running time.

This Twin Coach Model 34-S was restored by Monterey-Salinas Transit (MST) in Monterey, California. The bus was acquired in 1983 and restored by the MST maintenance department in eight months. It was painted in the colors of the Bay Rapid Transit Company, which had operated identical buses when that company operated transit service on the Monterey Peninsula. It was given the number 80, a fleet number of a similar Bay Rapid Transit Company bus bought in 1947. The Tacoma (Washington) Transit Company originally purchased the bus and later sold it to the Bremerton-Charleston (Washington) Bus Company, which retired it in 1983 after 35 years of service. It has been restored in the memory of the late Thomas D. Albert who managed Monterey-Salinas Transit between 1974 and 1982.

The late Dick Maguire of Harrisburg, Pennsylvania, owned this 1927 Fageol Safety Coach. He restored it after buying it from Werner Rosenquist, president of Empire Lines, Spokane, Washington. Rosenquist acquired it from the Auto Interurban Company when that company sold to Greyhound Lines.

Peninsula Charter Lines, East Palo Alto, California, has preserved this 1924 Fageol "streetcar" Safety Coach. It is reported to have originally operated with Pacific Electric Railway, Los Angeles, California.

The Manitoba Transit Heritage Association completed the restoration of this Model 23-R Twin Coach in 1989. This bus entered service in Winnipeg in 1937 and operated for 18 years.

This 1940 Twin Coach Model 41-GWFT was restored in 1989-1990 by the Metro Employees Historic Vehicle Association in Seattle, Washington, and is one of several vehicles restored by the organization since 1981. It is pictured at Route 2's scenic Medrona Park terminus, on the shore of Lake Washington, during a fan trip. The last of Seattle's 177 Twin Coach trolley buses was retired from service in January 1978.

Pierce County (Washington) Transit in Tacoma has this 1948 Model 41-S Twin Coach preserved. It was one of 33 buses delivered to the Tacoma Transit Company in March 1948.

The Verkehrsbetriebe Luzern in Luzern, Switzerland, originally purchased this Model 44-SDT Twin Coach in 1948. In the early 1970s the Stichting Veteraan Autobussen, a bus preservation group in Holland, acquired it. It has been painted to the livery of Maarse & Kroon, a Dutch bus company, which bought a fleet of Twin Coach buses in the late 1940s. *Wim Vink*

The Inter-City Model Safety Coach

THE FAGEOL SAFETY COACH is different from any other bus that has ever been placed on the market. This is because we have gone to work unhampered by conventions or preconceived notions as to bus design.

Our engineers spent months studying the needs of traction and bus companies, and with the facts gathered in this survey distinct in their minds they created a new type of vehicle, that from the ground up was designed for one purpose—passenger bus service.

While most of the motor busses made in the United States have been produced as sidelines in truck factories, or to a lesser extent by lengthening the chassis of touring cars, we have equipped our factory at Oakland, California, for the production of the specially designed bus which our engineers developed.

The Fageol Safety Coach, therefore, is a real bus made in a real bus factory, to meet the actual everyday needs of bus operators.

Our analysis shows what you have probably known for years, and what other manufacturers seem to have overlooked, or at least declined to take seriously—that the motor bus is an entirely separate class of motor vehicle.

Below are some of the salient points of the Inter-City model of the FAGEOL SAFETY COACH.

Body—Built in 20 and 23 passenger capacity. The distinguishing feature of the body is its lowness. The over all height is 6' 3-5/16" loaded. The floor is 19 inches off the ground. Head room has not been sacrificed to lowness, however. From the floor to the ceiling inside is 4' 5½".

Doors—The doors do not stop at the frame as in the conventional passenger car or bus but extend down to the running board as do also the body sides. Doors are limousine type, 27" wide and 53" high, extending to the top.

Ease of entrance and exit is obtained in the Safety Coach by the use of a wide running board, extending inside the doors and body sides. This feature invites persons of middle age to travel on stages, who otherwise would use other modes of transportation.

The neatness of the interior finish is evident from the careful treatment of the doors—the lower panel is pyramid aluminum, while that above is velour mohair fabric.

Running Board—The running board, which is 16" from the ground, does not stop at the edge of the body, but extends inside the doors for 3 or 4 inches. This gives ample width and extreme ease of entry or exit. The passenger is already inside the top before he steps from the running board to the floor.

Windows—Drop windows, which completely disappear into the doors or body sides, are provided. Lights are either plate glass or celluloid in metal frames,

at the buyer's option. Either style operates in felt grooves.

Framing—Body frame is of hardwood, all joints glued, and securely screwed or bolted. All covering is sheet aluminum.

Top—Top is of light slatted type with every cross slat glued and nailed. Over this is stretched canvas and then cotton batting and a final black, hard finish top covering.

Cowl—Substantial cast aluminum cowl extending from frame to ceiling gives stability, strength, and high class graceful appearance to the front of the body.

Windshield—One piece plate glass windshield is set in the cast aluminum cowl.

Ventilation—Great study has been given to ventilation to produce a car that will properly ventilate in all weather without being drafty. Two adjustable ventilators in front of the cowl and two more in the ceiling provide ample circulation in the winter, while all the side windows may be lowered into the body on hot days.

Interior Finish—Floor covered with linoleum, metal bound. Lower 8 inches of side wall covered with pyramid sheet aluminum, above this with durable fabric. The interior is airy and attractive in appearance, and is easily kept clean.

Lighting—The coach interior is well lighted without eye strain to the driver or passengers.

Two headlights are mounted in front between the fenders and radiator. A special illuminated sign board is provided above the windshield.

Luggage Space—A rear end baggage rack is regular equipment. Additional baggage space may be provided beside the driver in place of the regular cross seat at the option of the purchaser, making the capacity of the car 20 passengers instead of 23.

Upholstering—Genuine leather, overstuffed, on special spring construction, equal to that in the finest touring cars. Brown Spanish leather is standard equipment, but other colors are optional.

Paint—The Safety Coach is finished in Ry-enamel a wonderful new auto finish, which gives a semi-lustrous, tough, non-cracking surface. The enamel retains its original appearance for over a year, and can be renewed in 24 hours. Can be cleaned with water or gasoline. Colors optional.

A large baggage rack is built on the rear extension of the frame.

As the tires are 36x6 all round, it is necessary to carry only one spare, which slides into a special carrier beneath the baggage rack. It is locked in place by a quick-releasing lever clamp slotted for a padlock.

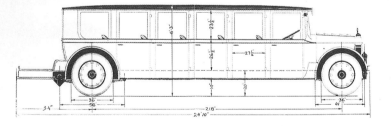

One of the first sales brochures of Fageol Motors came in 1922. It featured several pictures of the new Safety Coach, along with specifications and other information.

The Inter-City Model Fageol Safety Coach

GREATER profits through increased business and lower operating expense!"—This was the reason that more than a hundred operators have given for placing orders for additional Fageol Safety Coaches. In the inter-city model Fageol Safety Coach, the qualities that lead to this recognition of leadership in profits are very clearly seen.

The unmistakable safety of the coach, the beauty of the long, low lines and graceful proportions, the comfort and refinement of the interior, and the excellent service made possible by its dependability, are the qualities that have built up for this coach a degree of passenger popularity that is reflected in increased revenue wherever it is used.

Riding in this coach is a pleasure. The extreme lowness of the frame, together with the wide tread, transform the road motion into a gentle forward glide, with no hint of tossing or side sway. The seats are set at an angle that allows the passengers to relax, upholstering is much softer and more flexible than usual, and there is ample leg room even for very tall passengers. The engine carries the load so easily, and the road motion in the coach is so minimized, that fast schedules can be run without allowing the most timid passengers to become apprehensive on account of the speed—they simply do not realize how fast the coach is traveling.

The ability of the engine to get more miles out of a gallon of gasoline, its brute strength and unequaled pulling power, and the durability of the whole coach, have put the operating expense down to a point that is almost unbelievably low.

We build this coach in 22 passenger and 31 passenger capacities.

Below are some of the features that have given this coach its position of leadership.

Body—Limousine type, sheet aluminum over hardwood framing; completely enclosed; low, attractive lines. Overall height, 6' 7", loaded. Floor height, 22 inches from ground; running board, 16 inches, which makes

entrance and egress extremely easy. Headroom ample, 4' 6½". The wide doors extend all the way from the running board to the ceiling, a patented feature which adds to the low, safe appearance.

Windows—Plate glass, controlled by mechanical lifts, disappearing into the sides, so the coach can be completely closed in winter, or entirely open in summer.

Cowl—The one-piece cast aluminum cowl is designed to not only give a graceful appearance to the body, but also to take up the body strains, which reduces the wear and tear on the body and lowers the maintenance cost. A one-piece plate glass windshield is set in the cowl, and there are two ventilating windshields at the sides.

Ventilation—Great study has been given to the ventilation of the Fageol Safety Coach, so it will be airy at all times, yet not drafty or stuffy. Two adjustable ceiling ventilators provide for the intake of fresh air and the discharge of used air. As an auxiliary air supply, small trap-door ventilators are provided in the cowl.

Lighting—The coach interior is lighted with frosted glass dome lights set in the ceiling. A standard instrument board light is provided, so the driver may see all of the controls all the time. Two headlights are mounted on the front fenders, colored lights are attached to the upper corners of the cowl, and the standard tail light is accompanied by an electric stop warning.

Heaters—Special circulating heating system takes heated air off the manifold and distributes it through the coach.

Baggage Space—The space inside the body, back of the rear axle, is divided off for a baggage compartment, and fitted with regular passenger door. This can be easily and quickly loaded, and protects the baggage from the weather and from dust.

Compartments—A plate glass partition makes two separate compartments, making it possible to keep passengers likely to be objectionable out of the ladies' compartment, and providing a smoker where men will feel welcome.

Upholstering—Genuine leather seats, overstuffed, on special spring construction, equal to that in the finest touring cars. Standard material, brown Spanish leather. Wool mohair velour in ladies' compartment optional at a slight extra cost.

Interior Finish—Durable waterproof fabric on walls and ceiling, making cleaning easy. Bevel edge plate mirrors between window posts. Sheet aluminum on bottom 8 inches of sides and doors, for scuff plates. Floor covering, brown battleship linoleum, metal bound.

Outside Finish—Duco enamel, a wonderfully durable finish, holding its surface and color for a long time. Semi-lustrous, tough, and can be cleaned with warm or cold water, gasoline, or distillate. Colors optional.

Accessories—Standard equipment includes rear sight mirror; illuminated destination sign over windshield; automatic windshield wiper; a stop signal accessible from every seat in the coach, with no concealed wiring to get shorted; electric horn; front and rear bumpers; full set of tools, and 5-ton jack.

Wheels and Tires—Single Budd-Michelin steel disc wheels; front tires, 36 x 6 pneumatic; rear, 38 x 7 pneumatic. Spare wheel included. 36 x 6 dual tires on rear at extra cost.

Passengers appreciate the ease with which they can enter the FAGEOL SAFETY COACH.

The interior is arranged to please the passenger. A sliding plate glass partition makes two compartments. Heaters run through the entire length.

This enclosed baggage compartment saves time, and protects baggage from dust and from the weather.

The standard body finish is Duco enamel, which can be cleaned with a dry cloth without scratching, or washed with kerosene, gasoline, or distillate.

A page from one of the early Fageol Motors brochures (circa 1924) had excellent pictures of the new lengthened Safety Coach that was introduced.

The new Fageol Safety Coach was promoted with a variety of sales literatures, the covers of which are shown here.

Sutherland's Tijuana Stages
DISTRICT SOUTH OF SAN DIEGO

From Palm Trees To Snow Fields

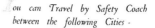

The

FAGEOL
SAFETY COACH

Brings Greater Profits

You can Travel by Safety Coach between the following Cities -

Oakland and Merced
Oakland to Sacramento via Vallejo
Sacramento to Stockton
Stockton to Oakland
   CALIFORNIA TRANSIT COMPANY
Oakland and San Jose
   PEERLESS STAGES
San Francisco and Santa Cruz
   AUTO TRANSIT COMPANY
Sacramento and Winters
   JUDY & ELLIOTT
Sacramento and Redding via West Side
   SHASTA TRANSIT COMPANY
Sacramento and Placerville
   PIERCE-ARROW STAGE COMPANY
Los Angeles and Santa Ana
   CROWN STAGES
Los Angeles and Murietta Hot Springs
   MURIETTA HOT SPRINGS STAGE LINE
San Diego and National City
   SAN DIEGO ELECTRIC RAILWAY CO.
San Diego and Tia Juana
   SUTHERLAND STAGE LINE
Denver, Colorado Springs and Pueblo
   INTER-CITY AUTOMOBILE LINES, INC.
Hibbing (Minnesota) and Duluth
   MESABA TRANSPORTATION COMPANY
Chicago, North Shore and Milwaukee Railroad—Chicago, Ill.
Street Car Service in Everett, Washington

DESIGNED AND MANUFACTURED BY

FAGEOL MOTORS COMPANY

OAKLAND, CALIFORNIA
PATENTS PENDING

Giving the public what it wants

Fageol Safety Coach brochures (1922-1927) were attractively designed. They advertised the benefits of the Safety Coach to bus company owners.

The Coach That Sells More Rides

Appearance   FAGEOL SAFETY COACH   *Performance*

NOW that motor bus transportation has become a stabilized public utility, offering a satisfactory and profitable means of transportation in connection with existing rail systems, and in several instances replacing the local electric transportation systems entirely, more and more traction men are turning to a study of the available equipment.

Getting down to basic principles, profitable bus transportation consists of just two things:
First; sell more rides.   Second; spend less per ride.

When you have accomplished the first you automatically achieve the second.

We built the FAGEOL SAFETY COACH to "sell more rides" for the operator. We knew that in order to accomplish this end, the passengers—both actual and prospective—must have the attitude of mind described by the merchandising man as "consumer acceptance." This state of mind is influenced mainly by two things: first, by appearance. The bus must be attractive, neat, clean and obviously safe. Second, by performance. It must be comfortable and easy riding. It must have power enough to maintain satisfactory running speeds, and ample braking facilities to handle the many stops, and keep the car under control at all times. It MUST be able to provide a reliable, consistant, steady service—the mechanical parts must be designed to withstand the strenuous service demanded of this class of vehicle.

We built the FAGEOL SAFETY COACH to fulfill these requirements—to "sell more rides." Experience has shown that in creating a vehicle which has demonstrated its ability to do these things we have also built a bus whose performance excells from the standpoint of economy.

FAGEOL SAFETY COACH "Type B" INTER-CITY MODEL

Fageol Safety Coaches are in great demand for school picnics and special trips, where the parents want to feel that their children are as safe as it is humanly possible for them to be.

"Every week end it is impossible to accommodate my trade. Everyone is anxious to ride in our bus. I am waiting for my second coach, which I hope you will ship as soon as possible, as I run in competition with two ——— busses."
From a letter written by John Donzelli, owner of the Golden Fawn, pictured above.

Manufactured by

FAGEOL MOTORS COMPANY
OAKLAND, CALIFORNIA

Better Equipment

More Profits

FAGEOL
SAFETY COACH

RANGE RAPID TRANSIT CO.

EVELETH, MINNESOTA

December 18th, 1923.

Fageol Motors Co.,
Oakland, California.

Gentlemen:

We purchased our first Fageol inter-city Safety Coach, Miss Minnesota, on October 15th, 1922, it being the first Fageol in this State. After operating it four weeks, we ordered our second Fageol Safety Coach, Miss Mesaba, it being delivered on the 6th of December, 1922. They were both put on the run between Duluth and Virginia, a distance of sixty-eight miles. We operated these two busses all through last Winter, each making two round trips daily, or 272 miles. We had all kinds of snow, and the two Fageols went through places that no other bus on the run could go through.

Mr. Art Lennartson, our driver on the Fageol, Miss Minnesota, went around the other busses and made his run. He still drives Miss Minnesota, and last Spring when we purchased more new Fageols and offered him one, he refused, saying that Miss Minnesota was good enough for him, claiming that through all kinds of roads and weather it had brought him home. Miss Minnesota to date has made 150,000 miles, while the second coach, Miss Mesaba, has made 130,000 miles.

We now own and operate five inter-city type Fageols, each making 272 miles per day, and three street car type Fageols between Virginia and Hibbing, Minnesota, each making 300 miles per day. We plan on replacing the balance of our busses with Fageols as soon as we can.

Other operators claimed at first that we would be tied up for parts. We have had wonderful service from your factory, getting anything ordered by wire in five days by express, and by wiring to Minneapolis in the morning, can get the parts by 10 o'clock p. m.

To sum the matter up in a few words, will say that your equipment has given us the greatest satisfaction, both from their attractive appearance and safety features and their great comfort, in being able to get the maximum in revenue, and from another source of utmost importance—low cost of operation.

Thanking you for your service and the interest you have shown in being of help to us, we remain,

Very respectfully,
RANGE RAPID TRANSIT COMPANY.
Per E. R. FITZGERALD.
Manager.

This is the first FAGEOL SAFETY COACH sold east of the Rocky Mountains. They now operate in more than twenty-nine states and three foreign countries.

A testimony by E. Roy Fitzgerald praised the Safety Coaches that were in the Range Rapid Transit fleet, presented in this 1923 Fageol Motors sales piece.

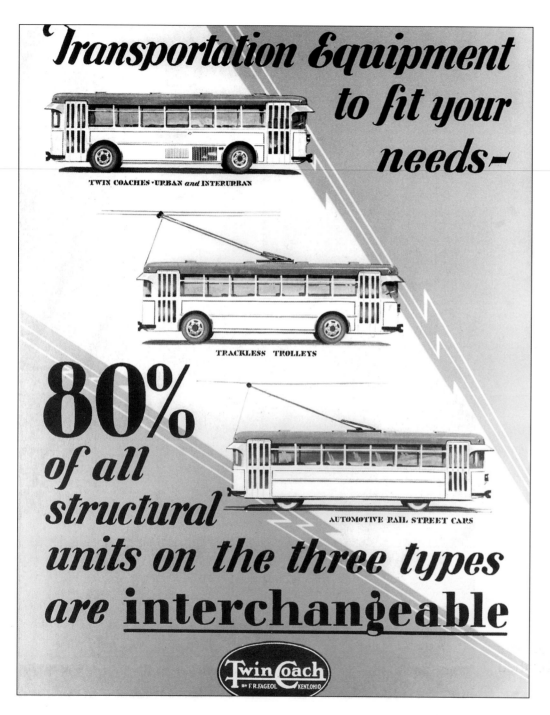

Transportation Equipment to fit your needs—

TWIN COACHES · URBAN *and* INTERURBAN

TRACKLESS TROLLEYS

AUTOMOTIVE RAIL STREET CARS

80% *of all structural units on the three types are* **interchangeable**

Twin Coach
BY F. R. FAGEOL KENT, OHIO

The Model 40 Twin Coach in the bus, trolley bus, and streetcar versions was advertised in a brochure of 1928, which featured this cover.

The smallest Twin Coach, the Model 15, was advertised with a full-color brochure published in 1933.

MODEL "15"   TwinCoach BY F.R. FAGEOL KENT, OHIO   17 PASSENGER

urban type **coaches**

AIRPORT — TWIN COACH

FAGEOL Twin Coach KENT · OHIO

TWIN COACH COMPANY
KENT, OHIO

Post-war Twin Coach buses were extensively described in a 44-page sales booklet issued in 1946.

The Model 58-D Super Twin Coach was promoted in a descriptive booklet sent to prospective customers in 1946.

In 1948, Twin Coach launched the Highway Luxury Liner with this brochure. It was unable to attract buyers. Only one Highway Luxury Liner was built.

In the early 1950s, the Twin Coach "Convertible" was introduced and this sales piece was issued to promote sales of the vehicle.

THE FAGEOL
Twin Coach "CONVERTIBLE"

• *New low cost, high utility vehicle* • *Easily converted from bus to cargo truck . . . or cargo truck to bus* • *May be operated as a combination bus and cargo vehicle* • *Gasoline or Propane Engine*

Fageol Twin Coach "Convertible"

• The Fageol Twin Coach "Convertible" brings an entirely new vehicle to the bus and truck fields.

As the name indicates, it can be converted at a moment's notice from passenger coach to cargo truck or vice versa. Or, it can be operated as a combination bus and cargo truck, transporting passengers comfortably, and, at the same time, carrying large quantities of freight and baggage.

Designed by L. J. Fageol, the "Convertible" offers all of the superior performance that has always distinguished Fageol Twin Coaches. Ideal for urban and intercity travel, it has many other military, civilian and industrial applications. It is indeed a truly modern vehicle, skillfully designed to meet today's transportation needs.

TWIN COACH COMPANY • KENT, OHIO

About the Author

When I first became interested in bus transportation in the 1930s, the Twin Coach name was very well known in the bus industry.

I became a subscriber to *Bus Transportation* magazine and through its pages I became more knowledgeable about the buses built by the Twin Coach Corporation. Twin Coach had some spectacular advertisements and there were interesting articles about Twin Coach as well. I wrote to the Twin Coach Corporation for literature and photographs. I was sent informative information and a number of photographs.

Duluth, Minnesota, where I was able to visit on numerous occasions, was an almost exclusive Twin Coach property. I noted that there were several different Twin Coach models in service in Duluth. They were the large Model 40s, along with Model 40 trolley buses used mainly on main routes. Models 23-R and 27-R Twin Coach buses were also in the fleet as well as the older Model S. I rode all of these Twin Coach models and I was quite impressed with them.

While I was in the service during World War II, I was stationed at several army installations. While at these locations I was able to visit a number of major cities and I can recall riding Twin Coach buses frequently in Little Rock, Miami Beach, and Raleigh as well as in eastern Massachusetts.

After I returned home, I became employed in the bus industry, and I did considerable traveling. At the time, the new post-war Twin Coach models were making their appearance in many places. I had the opportunity to see, ride and picture them in many cities throughout this country and Canada. Some of the cities on my itineraries were Milwaukee, Chicago, Kansas City, Green Bay, Winnipeg, San Antonio, Tucson, Phoenix, Los Angeles, and other places.

Unfortunately, the Twin Coach Corporation was not able to survive beyond the 1950s, but the buses produced by Twin Coach lasted for many years. A number of them have been preserved. I was able to picture many of the Twin Coach buses during my travels around this country and Canada. A good many of these pictures can be found on the pages of this book.

In my study of bus transportation, I feel that the Fageol brothers were among the leaders in the development of the bus industry. Their innovative designs and technologies helped bus companies grow and prosper. The Fageol brothers saw opportunities and acted at the right times.

It has been especially rewarding to produce this book, which pictures many of the interesting Fageol and Twin Coach models. Another bus history book, the *Bus Industry Chronicle*, which I recently wrote, has more pictures of Fageol and Twin Coach buses and historical information about the company.

I have had the opportunity to record additional bus industry history, especially with pictures, in several other books. These books are: *Greyhound Buses 1914-2000 Photo Archive*, *Trailways Buses 1936-1991 Photo Archive*, *Buses of Motor Coach Industries 1932-2000 Photo Archive*, *Yellow Coach Buses 1923-1943 Photo Archive*, and *Trolley Buses 1913-2001 Photo Archive*.

Bill Luke stands in front of a Duluth-Superior Transit Company Model 38-S Twin Coach when attending the Midwest Transit Association convention in Duluth, Minnesota, in August 1946.

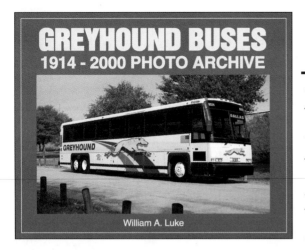
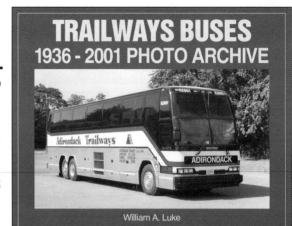

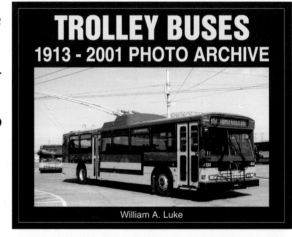

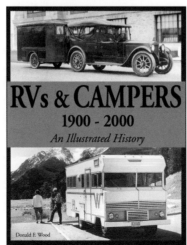
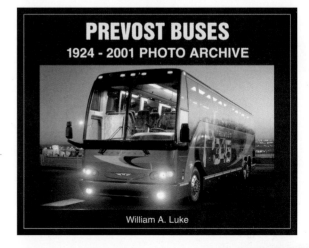